PERFORMANCE ESSENTIALS IN THE WORKPLACE

PERFORMANCE ESSENTIALS IN THE WORKPLACE

A Guidebook to **Inspire Action** and **Improve Results**

STEVE GILLILAND

Published by Advantage, Charleston, South Carolina.
Member of Advantage Media Group.

ADVANTAGE is a registered trademark and the Advantage colophon is a trademark of Advantage Media Group, Inc.

Printed in the United States of America.

ISBN: 978-1-59932-188-2
LCCN: 2010900218

This publication is designed to provide accurate and authoritative information in regard to the subject matter covered. It is sold with the understanding that the publisher is not engaged in rendering legal, accounting, or other professional services. If legal advice or other expert assistance is required, the services of a competent professional person should be sought.

Most Advantage Media Group titles are available at special quantity discounts for bulk purchases for sales promotions, premiums, fundraising, and educational use. Special versions or book excerpts can also be created to fit specific needs.

For more information, please write: Special Markets, Advantage Media Group, P.O. Box 272, Charleston, SC 29402 or call 1.866.775.1696.

Visit us online at **advantagefamily**.com

DEDICATION

To the many, many people who have so generously shared their experiences with me and inspired me to learn all I could about the prerequisites to performing at a high level.

To my wife Diane for her continued support and inspiration.

ACKNOWLEDGEMENTS

Special thanks to my director of marketing and information, my daughter-in-law, Amanda Gilliland, whose insights regarding organization and customer service have helped me while compiling this book.

Performance Essentials in the Workplace has also been deeply influenced by Sharon Alberts, a client and friend, whose level of commitment to improving performance in her organization has been an inspiration to me.

To James Barnett who gave me my start in the world of sales and marketing and gently but forcefully pushed me to strive for excellence and reach for new heights.

And a great deal of gratitude to everyone who has influenced me correctly regarding attitude, customer service, leadership, motivation, and teamwork.

In memory of Lou Gilliland, my father,

1932-2004

CONTENTS

WELCOME

This book was written because I couldn't find another one like it. I have attended many seminars, collected and written numerous workbooks, and read hundreds of books. Yet everything I have acquired doesn't condense the most important pieces of my training, the essentials we need to perform at a high level in the workplace.

As a professional speaker and author I have found that most of my clients spend more time talking about how to improve performance in the workplace than anything else. Through observations, interviews, and past work experience during a twenty five-year period, I have gathered practical information on techniques and methods for inspiring action and improving results. It was the absence of any integrated reference material, and repeated requests from many people who have heard me speak, that set me on the long course of putting this book together. Numerous people would ask for copies of my workbooks and then request permission to use the material back at their organizations. Of course my philosophy has always been, "share the riches."

This book is divided into chapters that provide a wealth of information on the five essentials necessary to performance in the workplace. Teamwork, motivation, attitude, organization, and customer service are vital to growth in the workplace, and critical to the survival of some companies. These five rudiments are either the organizations' best friends or their worst enemies. They are either intricate parts of the workplace culture, or the missing pieces that keep people and organizations from fulfilling their true mission and vision. These fundamentals are necessary for sales people, customer relations staff, engineers and scientists, bus drivers, teachers, police officers, nurses, volunteers, high school students, and of course, supervisors, managers, and executives in both public and profit making organizations.

In the pages that follow we will provide you with an overview of each performance essential plus numerous quotes to inspire you and your co-workers. Also a comprehensive workbook for each section provides a method for you to learn and includes a course outline to help train people in your organization. Your company may never achieve its desired culture; however, this book provides the means for doing it with more ease and greater success.

TEAMWORK

Achieving More Together

A diverse group formed each year to compete in a sport is an excellent example of team building. Groups develop into "teams" when their common purpose is understood by all of the members. Within effective teams each member plays an assigned role using his or her talent to the best advantage. When the members integrate their skills to accentuate strengths and minimize weaknesses, team objectives are usually achieved. When, on the other hand, groups play as individuals they usually fail. Most wins or losses are the result of "teamwork." In sports, feedback is often immediate. If teamwork is lacking, good managers can identify where the problems are and initiate corrective action in order to change things until the desired results are achieved.

Like their athletic counterparts, groups organized to perform business, community and government functions can achieve far more when they work as "teams." Unfortunately, many leaders fail to recognize and apply the same principles as when they would coach a sport. In a work organization they do not understand how to transform their group into a productive team. One reason may be that feedback in the form of results is not as quick and dramatic as in athletics. Problems can go unnoticed and corrective action if taken, can be slow in coming.

Effective teamwork knows no level. It is just as important among top executives, as it is among middle managers, first line supervisors or the rank and file. The absence of teamwork at any level, (or between levels) will limit organizational effectiveness and can eventually kill an organization. It requires effort to establish and maintain teamwork. If a leader does not place a high value on teamwork it will not occur. Teamwork takes a conscious effort to develop and continuous effort to maintain, but the rewards can be great when you begin *achieving more together.*

Commitment is a "no matter what" matter.

TEAM BUILDING BENEFITS

MEET THE DEMANDS OF THE NEW MILLENNIUM

1. Higher levels of performance
2. Greater customer satisfaction
3. Improved quality, service, and price
4. Pressure to continuously improve and be innovative
5. Increased competitiveness

SEIZE OPPORTUNITIES

1. Increase market share
2. Acquire new customers
3. Solve problems by drawing on the talents of a variety of individuals

> A successful team beats with one heart.

OVERCOME CHALLENGES

1. Turf battles
2. Decreasing productivity
3. Conflict is a daily occurrence
4. Communication is poor
5. Trust and cooperation are lacking
6. A merger or acquisition has occurred
7. A new team leader has been appointed
8. Reorganization or down-sizing
9. New responsibilities with no additional help
10. Apathy exists

IMPROVES THE ORGANIZATION

1. People
2. Attitude
3. Service
4. Meetings
5. Consistency
6. Communication
7. Creativity
8. Performance

> # Opportunities multiply when they are seized; they die when neglected

TEAM BUILDING MISTAKES

MOST COMMON MISTAKES

1. Recruiting
    a. Tendency: Hire people for what they know
    b. Result: Fire people for who they are
2. Leadership
    a. Tendency: Focus on improving systems
    b. Result: Doesn't develop people
3. Communication
    a. Tendency: Need-to-know basis
    b. Result: Confusion
4. Evaluations
    a. Tendency: Focus on individual performance
    b. Result: No reason to play as a team
5. Compensation
    a. Tendency: Based on tenure
    b. Result: No incentive to improve

FORM A TEAM FOR WEAK REASONS

1. To lighten the workload of the leader
2. To make workers transfer knowledge amongst one another to save on training costs
3. To determine the opinions and working styles of the staff
4. To get the staff to work harder

TEN CRITICAL MISTAKES

1. Failure to clearly define expectations
2. Failure to establish goals
3. Inattention to training
4. Lack of recognition
5. Failure to provide and receive feedback

6. Lack of involvement
7. Keeping those who don't respond to coaching
8. Permitting to exist negativity
9. Misunderstanding of responsibilities
10. Failure to nurture team building activities

KEY FACTORS THAT AFFECT A TEAM

1. Vision – mission and framework to get results
2. Leadership – effective, capable, and committed
3. Culture – norms that create a climate for excellence
4. Accountability – a way to monitor and improve team processes

> # Do what you value; value what you do

TEAM BUILDING CHALLENGES

CHANGING THE ATTITUDE

1. Believing in the mission
2. Creating the expectations
3. Defining accountability
4. Understanding the roles
5. Focusing on individual strengths

CATCHING THE VISION

1. Seeing it
2. Pursuing it
3. Achieving it
4. Helping others see it

MEETING COMMON PSYCHOLOGICAL NEEDS

1. The need to contribute
2. The need to feel competent
3. The need to achieve results
4. The need to be recognized and rewarded

SUSTAINING THE MOMENTUM

1. Trust
2. Enthusiasm
3. Focus
4. Commitment
5. Value

CREATING THE VISION

PROVISIONS

1. Ownership – what we create we support
2. Commitment – helps us see it through at all costs
3. Measurement – insight to see how well we are doing
4. Standard – a context for our decision making
5. Motivation – the reason we do what we do

PROCESS

1. Team member input
   a. Strengths
   b. Weaknesses
   c. Opportunities
   d. Threats
2. Create the objectives – what you will do
3. Design the tactics – how you will do it
4. Determine the resources – what you will need to do it
5. Assign the responsibilities – who will do it

Shared visions are the unifying force of a team

GOALS

1. Specific
2. Measurable
3. Achievable
4. Realistic
5. Timely

PLAN

1. Prioritize the objectives
2. Assign deadlines to every tactic
3. Monitor your progress

If you don't like what you're getting—
change what you're doing.

DEFINING THE PROCESS

ACCOUNTABILITY

1. Commonality – purpose
2. Expectations – roles
3. Responsibility – ownership
4. Accessibility – availability

MOTIVATION

1. Impact – why we do what we do
2. Contribution – value for what we do
3. Incentive – reward for what we do
4. Deadline – target to finish what we do

TRUST

1. Honesty – in every situation
2. Respect – earned
3. Honor – valuing other people
4. Unselfish – putting team first

INTEGRITY

1. Dependability – someone others can count on
2. Flexibility – anticipates and embraces change
3. Adaptability – sensitive to different types of people
4. Reliability – accurate information

DESIGNING THE TEAM

ASSESS STYLES

1. Dominant – tend to be a perfectionist, controlling, arrogant, competitive, focused, and passionate
2. Influential – tend to be persuasive, sociable, self-centered, convincing, charming, and outgoing
3. Balanced – tend to be patient, forgiving, impartial, choosy, restrained, and cautious
4. Loyal – tend to be humble, inflexible, other-centered, sentimental, content, and systematic

CLARIFY ROLES

1. What are your major job responsibilities?
2. What could others do to help you succeed at your job?
3. What could you do to help team members more?
4. Ideally, if you could redesign your job to more fully utilize your potential, minimize the most frustrating parts of your job, or motivate you more, what changes would you make?

People support what they help create.

DELIVER EXPECTATIONS

1. Positive
2. Enthusiastic
3. Responsive
4. Dependable
5. Compatible

DEVELOP SKILLS

1. Problem solving
2. Communication
3. Organization
4. Creativity

> A goal without a deadline is a dream.

COMMUNICATION ESSENTIALS

LISTENING

1. Distractions
    a. Personality conflict
    b. Content is boring
    c. Vocabulary
    d. Quality of voice
    e. Irritating mannerisms
    f. Hygiene and dress

2. Techniques
    a. Assertive position – be open
    b. Eye contact – fight distractions
    c. Take notes – gather information
    d. Listen for "feeling" words – intent vs impact
    e. Never interrupt – withhold judgment
    f. Clarify and verify – paraphrase and reflect

THREE FUNDAMENTAL FACTORS

1. Be honest and open
2. Feel and show respect
3. Communicate constructively

DELIVERING FEEDBACK

1. Be informed
2. Be concise
3. Be vulnerable
4. Be focused

RECEIVING FEEDBACK

1. Focus on the content and not the delivery
2. Remember the goal is long term
3. Control your emotions
4. Take notes
5. Be open to opportunities for improvement
6. Commit to action

> Teamwork is lending a hand
> not pointing a finger.

PERFORMANCE ESSENTIALS

TEAM PLAYERS - THE QUALITIES

1. Adaptable
2. Committed
3. Disciplined
4. Passionate
5. Positive

TRAINING - THE KNOWLEDGE

1. Technical skills
2. Soft skills
3. Continuous

COACHING - THE LEADER

1. Understanding – generational emotions and needs
2. Authenticity – revealing mistakes and weaknesses
3. Modeling – matching your actions with your beliefs
4. Attentive – being present for team members

EVALUATIONS - THE PLAN

1. Periodic assessment instead of annual review
2. Compensation based on performance, not cost of living
3. Objective, not subjective
4. Focus is on developing people first, then the bottom line

MEETING ESSENTIALS

REASON

1. Exchange information
2. Solve problems
3. Brainstorm new ideas
4. Educate
5. Develop plans and programs

PEOPLE

1. Leader – sets the objective
2. Sponsors – provide the agenda
3. Recorder – records the action plan
4. Timekeeper – monitors agenda
5. Facilitator – runs the meeting

AGENDA

1. Objective – clearly defined
2. Discussion items – provided by participants
3. Time limits – discussion items
4. Breaks – preassigned

A meeting with no agenda is
like a map with no cities.

CHECKLIST

1. Pre-meeting
    a. Distribute agenda a few days prior to the meeting
    b. Attach a memo to the agenda that includes the meeting objective, date, time, location, and attendees
    c. Encourage agenda sponsors to plan their parts
    d. Determine the cost

2. Meeting
    a. Begin on time
    b. Keep focused on objective and discussion items
    c. Maintain a parking lot
    d. Develop action plan
        i. Action
        ii. Person responsible
        iii. Deadline
    e. Summarize action plan and pass out meeting evaluation form
    f. Finish on time

3. Post-meeting
    a. Evaluations – returned within 24 hours
    b. Action plan – distribute to attendees within 3 days

COACHING THE TEAM

EMPOWER

1. Give team members the responsibility to do their job
2. Give team members the authority to make decisions
3. Give team members permission to fail

DELEGATE

1. Determine what needs to be done – the right thing
2. Determine who should do it – the right person
3. Share why it needs to be done – the importance
4. Share how it needs to be done – the training
5. Share when it needs to be done – the deadline

Brainstorm...someone already has the answer.

EQUIP

1. Evaluate them – how well did they do?
2. Qualify them – how well can they do?
3. Unite with them – how well can we do together?
4. Invest time in them – how can I personally help them?
5. Provide resources for them – how much better could they be?

DEVELOP

1. Develop self – become a survivor
2. Lead self – become a producer
3. Develop others – become a reproducer
4. Lead others – become a leader

TRAINING THE TEAM

TO IMPROVE THE TEAM, IMPROVE YOURSELF

1. Be teachable
2. Pick an area you want to improve
3. Plan your progress
4. Read books and periodicals in areas you want to become better
5. Attend a self development seminar every year

Charisma will get you in the door;
credibility will keep you there.

BOOKS

1. *Good To Great*, Jim Collins; HarperCollins Publishers, Inc.
2. *Quiet Strength*, Tony Dungy; Tyndale House Publishers, Inc.
3. *Timing is Everything*, Dennis Waitley; Thomas Nelson Publishers
4. *Laws of Teamwork*, John C. Maxwell; Thomas Nelson Publishers
5. *In-N-Out Burger*, Stacy Pearman; HarperCollins Publishers, Inc.
6. *It's Your Ship*, Captain D. Michael Abrashoff; Business Plus
7. *Loyalty Rules*, Frederick F. Reicheld; Harvard Business School Press
8. *Emotional Intelligence*, Daniel Goleman; Bantam Books
9. *Life Matters*, Philip C. McGraw, Ph.D.; Simon & Schuster
10. *The Pursuit of WOW*, Tom Peters; Vintage Books

EVALUATING THE TEAM

CUSTOMER SERVICE - INTERNAL AND EXTERNAL

1. Works to achieve internal and external customer satisfaction while meeting time, quality, and cost requirements
2. Treats every customer respectfully, courteously, and professionally
3. Keeps things simple and practical
4. Works to improve processes or procedures
5. Doesn't talk negatively about teammates

TEAMWORK AND ATTITUDE

1. Promotes the success of others
2. Supports decisions reached by the consensus
3. Communicates clearly
4. Exhibits flexibility and cooperation; willing to switch to other jobs or projects
5. Brings issues and/or conflicts to leadership

COMPANY SUCCESS

1. Works diligently to achieve desired results
2. Supports team guidelines and procedures
3. Is respectful of coworkers and leaders
4. Makes good use of resources and equipment
5. Responds favorably to required change

> If you're all wrapped up in yourself,
> then you're overdressed.

WORK HABITS AND QUALITY

1. Reports to work on time and as scheduled
2. Meets or exceeds standards of quality
3. Works in a safe manner
4. Maintains organized and neat work area
5. Performs work timely with minimal errors

Integrity is the agreement of our
actions with our beliefs.

PERSONAL ACTION PLAN

1. What impacted you the most in this chapter on Teamwork and how will it change the way you work with other people?

_____

_____

_____

_____

_____

2. Specifically, how & what are you going to do, based on #1 above?

_____

_____

_____

_____

_____

3. Who are you going to be accountable to?

_____

_____

_____

_____

_____

_____

The purpose of this action plan is to help make certain that by reading this chapter it produces a positive change in the way you approach team building.

Creating Your Edge

I love to tell the story about the chicken and the eagle. It's an old Indian fable about a young brave who took an egg from an eagle's nest and put it in a chicken's nest. When the egg hatched, the eagle thought he was a chicken. As the eagle grew up among the chickens, he learned their way of life. He pecked the ground for food, scratched the dust, and made vocal sounds like the chickens he lived with. One day he looked toward the sky and saw an eagle soaring above him. He flexed his wings and said to his mother, "I wish I could fly like that." "Don't be silly," his mother said, "you're a chicken; only eagles can soar so high in the sky." Feeling foolish and convinced his desire to fly was futile, the eagle went back to scratching and pecking in the dirt. He had, for all practical purposes, become a chicken – because he believed he was a chicken. Never again did he question his role on earth. It is all a matter of perception. When the eagle couldn't fly, it wasn't because he didn't have the natural ability, but rather because his belief was, "I am a chicken, and chickens can't fly." In order to fly, he needed to alter his perception of himself. He had to recognize his God-given abilities, and/or change his mindset concerning these abilities. He had to *believe!* Although our perceptions of reality determine what we believe, what we believe determines what we are and will become. Our *beliefs* determine our *expectations*, our expectations determine our *attitude*, our attitude determines our *behavior*, our behavior determines our *performance,* and our performance determines our *success*. As human beings, we tend to act appropriately to what we believe to be true, regardless of what is actually true or false. In other words, we are a product of conditioning in much the same manner that a computer is the product of its programming. What would you try to accomplish if you knew you wouldn't fail? It is time to change your beliefs about yourself and begin *creating your edge.*

Make your life a mission and never abort it.

ENJOY THE RIDE

TALENTS TO ENJOY THE RIDE

1. Passion
2. Energy
3. Enthusiasm

ELEMENTS TO SUSTAIN THE RIDE

1. Faith keeps you believing
2. Motivation keeps you moving
3. Love keeps you encouraged
4. Courage keeps you exploring
5. Wisdom keeps you safe

WHY PEOPLE ENJOY THE RIDE

1. Purpose
2. Reward

WHY PEOPLE DON'T ENJOY THE RIDE

Reasons	Solutions
Lack of enthusiasm	Motivation
Boredom	Challenge
Lack of interest	Empowerment
Cling to status quo	Involvement
No innovation	Security
Same thing too long	Development

BELIEVE IN YOURSELF

ROADBLOCKS

1. Low self-expectancy
2. Environment
3. Weak self-image
4. Lack of direction
5. Indecision
6. Lack of follow-through
7. Self-doubt
8. Lack of control
9. Identity awareness
10. Negative self-projection

DEFINING YOUR SELF-ESTEEM

1. Never take things personally
2. Never tie yourself to what you can't control
3. Never let anyone decide your worth
4. Never pity or belittle yourself
5. Never compare yourself to others

> An adventure is anything beyond
> your comfort level.

DEVELOPING YOUR SELF-ESTEEM

1. Build on your strengths
2. Acknowledge your weaknesses
3. Make yourself necessary
4. Learn something new every day

BELIEVING IN YOURSELF

1. Self-esteem
2. Patience
3. Perseverance

All motivation is self-motivation.

LEARN YOUR LIVING

WHY WE DON'T LEARN

1. Apathy—the message is never sought
2. Not smart enough—the message doesn't get through
3. Not paying attention—the message sails over our head
4. Not disciplined—the message gets in but not out

WHY WE CAN LEARN

1. We have the instructions
2. We have the experience
3. We have the choice

> A wish changes nothing.
> A decision changes everything.

WHO CAN HELP US LEARN

1. Mentor—someone who will teach us, advise us, and show us the way

2. Leader—someone whose excellence can be duplicated

3. Advocate—someone who believes in us

SELF-IMPROVEMENT RESOURCES

1. Books

2. Audios

3. Seminars

4. Periodicals

Become an expert in the impossible

PUT PEOPLE FIRST

TWO KINDS OF RELATIONSHIPS

1. Instrumental—exists to get something done
2. Social—exists for other reasons
   a. Superficial
   b. Intimate

INGREDIENTS OF A RELATIONSHIP

1. Love - unconditionally
2. Trust - honesty
3. Compassion - sensitivity
4. Commitment - involvement
5. Acceptance - diversity
6. Appreciation - gratitude

> Below your means, allows you
> to realize your dreams.

COMMUNICATING IN RELATIONSHIPS

1. Don't assume anything
2. Don't accuse
3. Focus on what is right, not who is right
4. Remember their perception is their reality

BUILDING POSITIVE RELATIONSHIPS

1. Value yourself
2. Resolve problems; don't endure them
3. Be who you are and appreciate who they are
4. Be good to your friends to keep them, and to your enemies to convert them
5. Don't judge because they aren't who they should be; pray they become who they could be

---

By chasing "there" you can't appreciate "here."

VALUE YOUR TIME

BE ACCOUNTABLE FOR YOUR TIME

1. Plan it
2. Protect it
3. Respect it

MINIMIZE YOUR TIME WASTERS

1. Interruptions
2. Lack of planning
3. Internet and email
4. Meetings
5. Disorganization

MAXIMIZE TIME SAVERS

1. Schedule your day
2. Delegate
3. Learn to say "no"
4. Over-communicate
5. Utilize peak time

REFOCUS YOUR ATTENTION

1. Family
2. Physical well-being
3. Emotional well-being
4. Career

MANAGE YOUR MONEY

THE BASIC PRINCIPLES

1. Stick to a budget
   a. Document your spending
   b. Budget all fixed expenses
   c. Keep your budget realistic
   d. Never shop without a list
2. Maximize retirement
   a. Insurance
   b. Investments
   c. Savings
3. Treat savings as a monthly expense
   a. 50% long term—retirement
   b. 30% emergency—the unexpected
   c. 20% emotional—the "wants"
4. Control your debt/income ratio
   a. Have only two credit cards
   b. Only borrow money for mortgage and/or auto loans

Comparison prohibits you from
seeing your uniqueness.

MANAGE YOUR MONEY

WARNING SIGNS - TOO MUCH CREDIT

1. Only making the minimum payment
2. Balances on credit cards are at the limit
3. Not enough cash to get through the month
4. Borrowing from one source to pay another
5. Worrying about money

REDUCE YOUR DEBT

CREDITOR	INTEREST RATE	PAYMENT	BALANCE	PAYOFF DATE
VISA	9.3%	75.00	800.27	04/07/04
TOTALS				

BUDGET YOUR MONEY

1. Build your credit
2. Understand your limits
3. Document your spending
4. Get the best deal
5. Expect the unexpected
6. Take action

Motivation has no limits

DRAW YOUR LINES

DEFINE YOUR LINES

1. What lines have I drawn?
2. What are my deadlines?
3. When I reach my lines, what else in my life will improve?
4. What resources do I need to reach my lines?

DRAW S.T.R.A.I.G.H.T. LINES

1. Specific
2. Timely
3. Realistic
4. Attainable
5. Interesting
6. Genuine
7. Healthy
8. Traceable

> Decide in your mind but
> choose from your heart.

REACH FOR YOUR LINES

1. Compete against yourself
2. Reward yourself
3. Stretch yourself
4. Reassure yourself

GO ABOVE YOUR LINES

1. Stay focused
2. Make sacrifices
3. Keep on your toes

Desire more than you can accomplish

REDEFINE YOUR LUCK

DEVELOP YOUR PLAN

1. Opportunities
    a. Discernment to recognize them
    b. Motivation to act on them
    c. Determination to seize them
2. Obstacles
    a. Courage to confront them
    b. Strength to overcome them

BE F.A.M.O.U.S. WITH YOUR PLAN

1. Flexible; be ready for change
2. Adaptable; be sensitive to differences
3. Masterful; be extraordinary at something
4. Optimistic; look for the positive in everything
5. Unselfish; give more than you take
6. Steadfast; stay committed to the plan

BE OPEN TO ALL POSSIBILITIES

1. Strive for perfection—don't plan for mediocrity
2. Push the limit—you get 0% of what you don't pursue
3. Risk success—don't fail by never trying

MATCH YOUR HABITS TO YOUR PLAN

1. Destructive
2. Constructive

COMMIT TO ACTION

ACTION REQUIRES DISCIPLINE

1. Hard work
2. Stamina
3. Character

DISCIPLINE REQUIRES COMMITMENT

1. Interest – you only do things when it is convenient
2. Vow – is an obligation; you accept no excuses, only results

COMMITMENT REQUIRES INITIATIVE

1. Initiative is not what we think
2. Initiative is not what we know
3. Initiative is not what we believe
4. Initiative is not what we say
5. Initiative is what we do

Enjoying the ride makes success priceless.

INITIATIVE REQUIRES ACTION

1. Start the process: don't fear what you want the most
2. Unlock your potential: give up what you are to receive, what you can become
3. Create your own reality: dare to be different
4. Choose your attitude: no one can ruin your day without your permission
5. Expect challenges: a path with no problems leads nowhere
6. Show up every day: always perform at your highest level
7. Stay in the game: success stops when you do

Motivation is going ahead without success.

PUNCTUATE THE POSITIVE

YOUR ATTITUDE IS EVERYTHING

1. The librarian of your past

2. The speaker of your present

3. The prophet of your future

YOUR ATTITUDE REVEALS YOUR RESPONSE

1. Negative
   a. Pessimistic
      i. Distorts the picture
      ii. "What if" belief system
   b. Unrealistic
      i. Reactive to problems
      ii. Takes on everything; accomplishes nothing
      iii. Expects something for nothing

2. Positive
   a. Optimistic
      i. Sees the bigger picture
      ii. "I can" belief system
   b. Realistic
      i. Anticipates obstacles
      ii. Understands limitations
      iii. Improves continuously

FACTORS THAT INFLUENCE YOUR ATTITUDE

1. Past mistakes
2. Present circumstances
3. Future fears
4. Unforeseen problems
5. Relationships
6. Change

YOUR INTAKE AFFECTS YOUR OUTLOOK

1. What we read
2. What we watch
3. What we hear
4. Who we're with

> Every little quit hurts.

VISUALIZE TO REALIZE

RISK BEING FIRST

1. Courage
2. Confidence
3. Creativity

PREPARE TO SEE THE HORIZON

1. Glasses – correct your vision
2. Binoculars – bring your vision closer
3. Windshield Wipers – clear the obstruction from your vision
4. Microscope – see below the surface of your vision
5. Flashlight – enlighten your vision
6. Sunglasses – remove the glare from your vision

Every day is a gift from God, that's
why it's called the present.

SEE BEYOND THE HORIZON

1. If you don't know, go find out
2. When you make a mistake, admit it
3. Don't avoid problems, go through them
4. Don't make promises, make commitments
5. Never be content with how good you are
6. Learn from those who are superior
7. Always look for a better way to do it

MOVE BEYOND YOUR COMFORT ZONE

1. Discover more
2. Learn more
3. Affirm more

Extraordinary people JUST over DO IT.

REFUSE TO QUIT

ACKNOWLEDGE YOUR FEELINGS

1. Realize quitting is a natural feeling
2. It's okay to express your feelings
3. Don't give in to the feelings of quitting
4. Base your feelings on today
5. Ignore those who try to influence your feelings negatively
6. Your feelings are unique to your situations

CONTROL YOUR DECISIONS

1. Never make any decision when you are experiencing a shift in emotion
2. Recruit others to help make your decisions
3. Always remember quitting is a permanent decision

Flexibility is when "what is" evolves immediately into "what was."

EMBRACE YOUR ADVERSITY

1. Learn from it
2. Grow because of it
3. Change as a result of it

REMEMBER YOUR MENTORS

1. **Fred Astaire**

   After his first screen test in 1933, MGM testing director said, "Can't act. Slightly bald. Can dance a little."

2. **Vince Lombardi**

   An expert said, "He possesses minimal football knowledge. Lacks motivation."

3. **Walt Disney**

   Was fired by a newspaper for lacking ideas. He also went bankrupt several times.

4. **Ludwig Beethoven**

   His teacher called him a hopeless composer.

> Growth is the process of failing
> to ultimately succeed.

PERSONAL ACTION PLAN

1. What impacted you the most in this chapter on Motivation and how will it help you create your edge?

    _____

    _____

    _____

    _____

    _____

    _____

2. Specifically, how & what are you going to do, based on #1 above?

    _____

    _____

    _____

    _____

    _____

3. Who are you going to be accountable to?

    _____

    _____

    _____

    _____

    _____

    _____

The purpose of this action plan is to help make certain that by reading this chapter it produces a positive change in the way you create your edge.

Dealing With Negativity

Most of us are so geared towards the negatives of life that we agree with George Carlin, the comedian, who jokes that "Positive thinking is miscalculation." We come to believe that surely the world was not organized for good. We convince ourselves that it was not organized for our good. Those who believe the world was capitulated to evil naturally believe it would be a "miscalculation" to anticipate good for themselves.

Positive thinking is not miscalculation. I've found it to be the way life works best. Positive thinking is more important to us than we know. Dr. Norman Vincent Peale once pointed out that it takes ten positives to overcome one negative. We need as many positives in our lives as we can get! When we begin to look beyond our personal scars and focus on our stars, we find we are starting to think and act positively. I've discovered that when I can be positive, even toward negative situations, positive results occur. Positive results, of course, move us forward. Positive thinking about our goals, our dreams, our aspirations helps us to go for the max and live a more fulfilling life.

Call this philosophy anything you choose. Call it *positive thinking, possibility thinking*, or a *positive mental attitude*. Whatever term we choose, it means thinking, acting, and reacting *affirmatively*. It means thinking positively in love and faith, not negatively in fear and distrust of other people, circumstances, happenings, and life events. In order to deal with negativity we must begin with ourselves. Easy to say, but I've found I really have to work at it. Negativity is all around us. I find I must focus my thoughts towards healthy, positive ends. It's easy to talk the talk, hard to walk the walk. Meanwhile, I try to fast from negativity and practice a positive approach to my challenges. I've found that positive thinking really works when *dealing with negativity.*

Positive action always brings positive results.

DEFINING NEGATIVITY

WHERE IT BEGINS - CHILDHOOD

1. Abandonment – feeling unwanted
2. No stability – irresponsibility
3. No limits – inability to say "no"
4. Avoidance – need to be liked outweighs need to confront
5. Discipline – control or out of control
6. Attention – needs excitement, chaos, or drama

HOW IT OCCURS - CONTRADICTORY EXPECTATIONS

1. Taking risks	Being correct
2. Being decisive	Being participative
3. Being ambitious	Being loyal to a company
4. Taking charge	Being a team player
5. Personal goals	Organizational goals

Enthusiasm makes everything different.

WHY IT CONTINUES

1. Habitual thinking makes it normal to focus on wrong
2. Cultures accept it
3. We tolerate it
4. It sells – sensationalism
5. It naively elevates self-esteem
6. It subtly gets in
7. It gets attention

WHAT IT COSTS

1. Productivity
   a. Substandard performance
   b. Morale
   c. Deadlines aren't met
2. Quality
   a. Mistakes increase
   b. Average is accepted
   c. Confidence is lost
3. Wasted resources
   a. People – potential
   b. Time
   c. Money

UNDERSTANDING HUMAN BEHAVIOR

HOW WE GET THE WAY WE ARE

1. Biology
   a. Genetics
   b. Present physiological characteristics
2. Environment
   a. Caught and taught behaviors
   b. Parents or parental figures
   c. Role models, friends, and idols
   d. Cultural conditioning
   e. Societal values
   f. Training and education
   g. Experiences
   h. Circumstances (past and present)
3. Personal choices
   a. Behaviors, decisions, and beliefs
   b. Constructive choices – responsible and helpful
   c. Unconstructive choices – irresponsible and harmful

Replace all negatives with positives.

THE BEHAVIORAL CHAIN REACTION

1. Stimuli
2. Thoughts
3. Actions
4. Habits
5. Character
6. Life Path

CHANGING HUMAN BEHAVIOR

1. Willingness to learn and grow
2. Awareness of the need for change
3. Incentive to change
4. Commitment to change
5. Realistic plan for changing
6. Support and encouragement
7. Accountability
8. Constructive feedback on progress
9. Opportunity to learn from mistakes
10. Reasonable consequences for continued noncompliance

> Attitudes are contagious. Be a carrier.

HELPING OTHERS TO CHANGE

1. Care – show you have a genuine desire to be helpful
2. Make aware – discuss the issues openly and honestly
3. Understand – listen and understand without condoning or judging
4. Reason – evaluate present choices and possible constructive alternatives and the consequences of continuing old behavior
5. Develop commitment to change – explore what a person is willing to own responsibility for doing

AVOID NEGATIVE STIMULI

1. Relationships
2. Information

REFOCUS YOUR ATTENTION

1. Important
2. Urgent

Problem solving starts with a positive outlook.

VALUE OTHER PEOPLE

1. Have an attitude of genuine caring
2. Actively listen and demonstrate interest
3. Focus on problems, not people
4. Be honest
5. Assume the best about people
6. Practice patience and self-control
7. Constructively express your feelings

PURSUE THE POSITIVE

1. Maintain a childlike innocence
2. Accept life on life's terms
3. Guard your self-talk
4. Burn your bridges
5. Make a difference

Attitude doesn't solve problems, it
only determines the outcome.

IDENTIFYING NEGATIVE BEHAVIOR

UNREALISTIC

1. Perfectionist
    a. Identifying Feature: Lack of tolerance and patience
    b. Root Cause: Insecure
2. Procrastinator
    a. Identifying Feature: Overwhelmed
    b. Root Cause: Disorganized
3. Workaholic
    a. Identifying Feature: Career is #1 priority
    b. Root Cause: Fear of losing control

UNDISCIPLINED

1. Spoiled
    a. Identifying Feature: Nothing is ever good enough
    b. Root Cause: Discontent
2. Autonomous
    a. Identifying Feature: Never takes responsibility
    b. Root Cause: Not afraid of consequences
3. Coddled
    a. Identifying Feature: Repeat same mistakes
    b. Root Cause: No consequences

IDENTIFYING NEGATIVE BEHAVIOR

DISRUPTIVE

1. Cynics
   a. Identifying Feature: Nothing will ever work
   b. Root Cause: Not empowered
2. Instigators
   a. Identifying Feature: Gossiping and positioning
   b. Root Cause: Lack self-confidence
3. Whiners
   a. Identifying Feature: Chronic complaining
   b. Root Cause: Seeking attention

DORMANT

1. Resisters
   a. Identifying Feature: Likes status quo
   b. Root Cause: Never had to change
2. Compromiser
   a. Identifying Feature: Settles for less
   b. Root Cause: Lack self-esteem
3. Apathetic
   a. Identifying Feature: Doesn't care
   b. Root Cause: Sees no value

RESPONDING TO NEGATIVE BEHAVIORS

UNREALISTIC

1. Perfectionist
   a. Reassure them
   b. Recognize them
2. Procrastinator
   a. Don't give them more than they can handle
   b. Assign deadlines
3. Workaholic
   a. Don't compromise your own priorities
   b. Encourage family and leisure time

UNDISCIPLINED

1. Spoiled
   a. Don't give in to their wants
   b. Reason with reality
2. Autonomous
   a. Hold them accountable
   b. Provide support and encouragement
3. Coddled
   a. Communicate the impact
   b. Explain possible consequences

Anger is only one letter short of danger.

DISRUPTIVE

1. Cynics
   a. Make them part of the process
   b. Give them permission to fail
2. Instigators
   a. Refuse to tolerate
   b. Confront
3. Whiners
   a. Don't give in or join in
   b. Make them feel valued

DORMANT

1. Resisters
   a. Show them the benefits
   b. Help them to visualize the end result
2. Compromiser
   a. Challenge them
   b. Encourage them
3. Apathetic
   a. Provide a reason to care
   b. Show them you care

Doubt your doubts, not your beliefs.

INFLUENCING NEGATIVE BEHAVIOR

CULTIVATE RICHER RELATIONSHIPS

1. Be vulnerable – admit your fears and shortcomings
2. Stop making negative assumptions
3. Stop being so critical
4. Get more involved – care enough to know, know enough to care
5. Be willing to change first

PRACTICE BEING AGREEABLE

1. Apologize when appropriate
2. Be willing to talk about issues
3. Acknowledge their viewpoint
4. Recognize good points

BE OPEN TO THEIR THOUGHTS AND FEELINGS

1. Always be fair and equitable
2. Practice participation, not dictation
3. Think of what they want
4. Respect their perception
5. Don't argue your opinion

SET THE RIGHT EXAMPLE

1. Always deal with the facts
2. Practice being outstanding
3. Communicate openly and honestly
4. Match your actions to your beliefs

DEFUSING ANGER

THE SOURCE OF ANGER

1. Activating event – something is altered or changed
2. Belief system – the alteration or change is opposite our conviction or opinion
3. Response system – our biological, environmental, and personal choices we have been imprinted with trigger us
4. Consequences – depending on the consequence, if any, determines our willingness and degree of response

CALMING TECHNIQUES

1. Value their opinion
2. Expect their emotion
3. Nurture their ego
4. Transfer their energy

Enough white lies will make you go color blind.

REDUCE DEFENSIVENESS

1. Listen
2. Avoid the A.D.R. cycle
    a. Accuse
    b. Defend
    c. Re-accuse
3. Offer suggestions rather than disagreeing
4. Mirror their feeling

USE TACT

1. Talk
2. After
3. Careful
4. Thinking

> Keep your heart right even when
> it is sorely wounded.

RESOLVING CONFLICT

REASONS FOR CONFLICT

1. Personality differences
2. Organizational culture
3. Values
4. Goals
5. Job descriptions
6. Perception
7. Communication
8. Baggage
9. Policies and procedures
10. Available resources

CONFLICT CAN BE POSITIVE

1. Enhances relationships
2. Increases productivity
3. Promotes growth and learning
4. Achieves goals

> Love is forgiving; commitment is forgetting.

CONFLICT STYLES

1. Avoidance
2. Accommodation
3. Compromise
4. Dominate
5. Collaboration

CONFRONT ASSERTIVELY

1. Express your feelings
2. Communicate the impact
3. Validate the concern
4. Ask for solutions
5. Agree on a direction
6. Deliver the consequences
7. Commit to the individual

Attitude is accepting and
embracing life's challenges.

COPING ESSENTIALS

PATIENCE

1. Control your emotions during a confrontation
2. Make decisions based on accurate and complete information and not solely on the opinions of others
3. Do not deliver ultimatums prematurely whenever a problem arises in an effort to solve it quickly

AWARENESS

1. Don't ignore the problem hoping it will eventually go away
2. Don't assume the problem is an isolated occurrence

CONSISTENCY

1. Focus on problems, not personalities
2. Confront in private
3. Be sure your motive is honorable

COMMUNICATION

1. Listen to their side of the issue
2. Don't make assumptions regarding their feelings
3. Ask them instead of telling them
4. Focus on what is right, not who is right

REDUCING STRESS

STRESS-PRODUCING BEHAVIORS

1. Complaining – nothing is ever right
2. Indecisive – can't make decisions
3. Inflexible – rejecting anything new
4. Couching – always sitting at home, tending to be fatigued, and pulse rate increases
5. Disorganization – "so what" attitude
6. Self-centered – rebellious and can't handle criticism
7. Scapegoat – blaming others or circumstances for your problems
8. Apathetic – playing the role of the victim
9. Impatient – it has to be now
10. Overindulgence – too much eating, drinking, smoking, or any other stimuli that can be destructive if not moderated

MOST COMMON STRESS-PRODUCING CIRCUMSTANCES

1. Perfectionism – every responsibility has to be perfect and completed
2. Guilt – you aren't meeting the expectations of others
3. Change – you fear the outcome
4. Relationships – you anticipate unpleasant encounters and/or conflict
5. Finances – too much debt and not enough money
6. Job – inconsistent workload, unclear expectations, monotonous tasks, inadequate communication and leadership

DAILY CHECKLIST TO REDUCE STRESS

1. Go to bed early – become a morning person
2. Eat a well-balanced diet – stay energized
3. Take a walk – maintain your metabolism
4. Spend ten minutes of quiet time – reboot your brain
5. Take your breaks and lunch hours – don't cheat yourself
6. Do something fun – play
7. Try something new – learn to let go
8. Set limits – learn to say "no"
9. Go home on time – never forget what's important
10. Have a support person – keep encouraged

KEYS TO HANDLE STRESS

1. Identify your stressors – handle the truth
2. Minimize your stressors – life rewards action
3. Assign the right value to circumstances
4. Be honest in everything

Success is being happy, not right.

KEEPING BALANCE

INTERNAL BALANCE

1. Mental
2. Emotional
3. Physical
4. Spiritual

EXTERNAL BALANCE

1. Family
2. Work
3. Play
4. Relationships
5. Social life
6. Financial
7. Activities

When the past tries to dominate your
thoughts, let your dreams ignite your day.

INTERNAL RESOURCES

1. Expose our mind to constructive inputs
2. Willingness to know, process, and express our feelings rationally and constructively
3. Physical fitness
   a. Exercise
   b. Diet
4. Loving others and self in the harmony in our life combined with the depth of our wisdom and correctness of our beliefs

EXTERNAL RESOURCES

1. Loving unconditionally
2. Loving what you do, why you do it, and who you do it with
3. Taking time to have fun
4. Loving like you have never been hurt
5. Dancing like no one is watching
6. Realizing abundance is the result of appreciation, not accumulation
7. Learning how to relax

> You will never leave where you are until you decide where you would rather be.

CHANGING YOUR PATH

STIMULUS

1. Internal things that cause a response
2. External things that cause a response

RESPONSE

1. Thoughts – interact with our emotional and physical system to produce actions. Constructive thoughts lead to constructive actions. In this context, *constructive* means responsible, self-developing, and mature. The word *unconstructive* means irresponsible, self-defeating, and immature.

2. Actions – tend to be consistent with our thoughts. Inconsistencies may be controlled by subconscious thoughts, our emotions, or our physical system and tend to result in inner tension. Actions that are practiced become habits. Constructive actions lead to constructive habits.

> Your day goes the way the
> corners of your mouth go.

CONSEQUENCES

1. Habits – practiced thoughts, feelings, and actions. Our habits shape our character. Constructive habits lead to the development of a healthy, strong character.

2. Character – our mental, emotional, physical, and spiritual characteristics as a whole person. Our character shapes our life path.

3. Life Path – long-term behavioral patterns, our life style (including our priorities, goals, and activities), and our destiny as a winner or loser. A change in character will produce a change in our life path by affecting our behavioral patterns, life style, or destiny.

END RESULTS

Our responses and the constructive, unconstructive, or neutral consequences that they may have on our habits, character, and life path result in outcomes that may affect future stimuli or responses.

> Extraordinary people discuss ideas,
> ordinary people discuss events, and
> shallow people discuss people.

PERSONAL ACTION PLAN

1. What impacted you the most in this chapter on Attitude and how will it change the way you deal with negativity in the workplace?

_____

_____

_____

_____

_____

_____

2. Specifically, how & what are you going to do, based on #1 above?

_____

_____

_____

_____

_____

_____

3. Who are you going to be accountable to?

_____

_____

_____

_____

_____

_____

The purpose of this action plan is to help make certain that by reading this chapter it produces a positive change in the way you deal with negativity in the workplace.

Managing Multiple Priorities

As far back as the early 1900's, Victor Pareto explained why a priority system was so important in securing effectiveness. As you recall, his rule, when applied to setting priorities, states that 80 percent of the value of a group of items is generally concentrated in only 20 percent of the items. In other words you can be 80 percent effective by achieving 20 percent of your goals. If you have a daily action list of ten items, you can expect to be eighty percent effective by successfully completing only the two most important items on the list. To be effective you must concentrate on the most important items. You must make a commitment to your commitment to focus on true priority items.

At the beginning of every day, I rank the five most important things I have to do. Then I go to work on number one, and continue to work until I am finished. When I finish the first task, I reevaluate the other four items to make sure nothing has changed in the ranking. I then go to work on number two. When it's done, I reevaluate, and then work on number three. If the day ends and I haven't finished all five, I never worry. I wouldn't have got all five done using any other method either. I did, in fact, do the most important thing on my list (which today was writing this chapter).

Even if the day goes by and I don't even finish number one, I always remind myself that I was still working on the most important thing. The secret is to choose what's most important to you and do it first. It's that simple. The hard part is deciding what is most important. Goethe said, "Things which matter most must never be at the mercy of things which matter least." E.M. Gray spent his life searching for the one common denominator that all successful people share. He found it wasn't hard work, good luck, or astute human relations, though those were all important. The one factor that seemed to transcend all the rest was putting first things first to be successful at *managing multiple priorities.*

> # Abundance is a result of appreciation not accumulation.

MANAGING YOUR PURPOSE

DEFINE YOUR PURPOSE

1. Goals
2. Plan
3. Rewards

DEFINE YOURSELF

1. Self-acceptance
2. Self-esteem
3. Self-respect
4. Self-pleasing

CREATE YOUR OWN REALITY

1. No one can ruin your day without your permission
2. Decide to be happy
3. Success stops when you do
4. When your ship comes in, be willing to unload it
5. Give life's precious moments value – share them
6. Don't fear what you want the most
7. Make yesterday the deadline for all complaints
8. Look for opportunities, not guarantees
9. Make now the most interesting time of all
10. When things go wrong, don't go with them

FOCUS ON N.O.W.

1. Never look back
2. Others can't stop you
3. We will never have it all together

MANAGING YOUR ATTITUDE

CONCERNING CHANGE

1. Awareness – your ability to identify issues and behaviors that need to be changed
2. Acknowledgment – admitting you need to make a change
3. Willingness – the ability to move from believing you should change to desiring and choosing to change
4. Strategy – the tactical plan to deliver the change
5. Accountability – a person who will hold you to changing and monitor your progress
6. Perseverance – your ability to hold on

CONCERNING FORGIVENESS

1. Toward yourself
   a. What was your intent
   b. What will you do different the next time
   c. Move forward and don't look back
2. Toward others
   a. Allow yourself to express your feelings
   b. Examine their intent – look beyond the impact
   c. Be compassionate – care
   d. Move forward and don't look back

A "will be" is a "has been" in progress.

CONCERNING FAILURE

1. Welcome the lessons - they precede success
2. Focus on your strengths
3. Acknowledge your limitations
4. Cancel your "pity parties"

CONCERNING THE FUTURE

1. Stimuli
   a. External
   b. Internal
2. Responses
   a. Thoughts
   b. Actions
3. Consequences
   a. Habits
   b. Character
   c. Life Path

Never complain about what you permit.

MANAGING YOUR STRESS

FIVE WAYS TO COMBAT JOB STRESS

1. Don't react, act—Identify the underlying issue. Try to stay objective, especially if other people are involved. Use friends, trusted co-workers and others who may have a valuable perspective to help analyze the situation and identify the basic issues.

2. Take control—Again, use carefully selected friends and co-workers to help define and reinforce the course of action. The key is to do something.

3. Learn effective communication skills

    a. Organize thoughts and key points

    b. Express ideas clearly and logically

    c. Objectively identify the fundamental stress issues

    d. Identify a solution or course of action

    e. Identify the benefits to your superior and the company

4. Create a means to combat boredom—Learn why your job is necessary, how it contributes to the company's overall growth and quality of the products.

5. Know what you like about your job—Figure out how to involve yourself in those aspects, either by volunteering for additional responsibilities, seeking additional training or transferring to another department. If you don't like anything about the job, consider changing jobs.

TAKE CHARGE

1. Implement a stress-free diet

    a. Eat foods that will combat stress such as citrus fruits or other sources of vitamin C

    b. Avoid foods that aggravate stress such as deep-fried foods high in fat

2. Manage stress through relaxation

3. Work out stress through exercise

BALANCE CAREER AND FAMILY

1. Decide what's important—You have to agree on work and home priorities, both individually and as a family. This will, no doubt, involve making difficult choices, many of which involve money.

2. Set limits—You can't do it all and neither can your partner. So set limits and discuss them so that expectations are realistic.

3. Learn when to say "no"—Say "no" when a request or demand is made that conflicts with priorities or exceeds limits that have been set.

4. Don't give in to guilt—If you've defined priorities and limits objectively and are willing to stay flexible and cooperative with your partner, there is no reason to feel guilty.

COMBAT FINANCIAL STRESS

1. Check your priorities and expectations—Are you trying to create an unrealistic (and unaffordable) lifestyle? Why?

2. Establish a budget—If you can create a balanced budget, it becomes an impartial means for settling future spending disputes. (The budget, not individual preferences or impulse, then dictates spending decisions.)

3. Create a savings program—Having money tucked away is insurance against future financial stress should a job loss, emergency, illness or home repair occur.

Anytime you spend time doing something someone else can do, you won't have time to do what only you can do.

MANAGING YOUR RELATIONSHIPS

THROUGH LOVE

1. Acceptance
2. Support
3. Patience
4. Unconditional

THROUGH TRUST

1. Honesty
2. Integrity
3. Respect
4. Honor

THROUGH APPRECIATION

1. Appreciate their interests
2. Appreciate their differences
3. Appreciate their contributions
4. Appreciate their efforts

THROUGH FOCUS

1. On "what" is right
2. Not "who" is right

> Become addicted to continuous
> self-improvement.

MANAGING YOUR ACTIVITIES

VALUE YOUR TIME

1. Schedule it – take 15 minutes to plan your day
2. Maximize it – identify your peak productivity time
3. Respect it – reduce time wasters
4. Protect it – utilize time savers

REDUCE TIME WASTERS

1. Interruptions – telephone and drop-in visitors
2. Lack of goals and planning
3. Message retrieval – voice mail and email
4. Meetings
5. Disorganization
6. Internet
7. Bureaucracy – peers and boss
8. Lack of self-discipline
9. Television
10. Crisis management

> Courage is being scared and then doing the thing you think you can't do.

UTILIZE TIME SAVERS

1. Plan your day

2. Delegate

3. Learn to say no

4. Never assume

5. Maximize your peak time

END PROCRASTINATION

1. Recognize you have a problem

2. Do something – it's better than nothing

3. Break tasks into small action steps

4. Set a deadline

5. Avoid perfectionism

6. Avoid over-commitment

7. Do it now

Elevation is the act of reaching down.

MANAGING YOUR SPACE

INVENTORY – ONE SPACE AT A TIME

1. Personal – home
    a. Storage
        i. Closets
        ii. Garage
        iii. Attic
        iv. Basement
    b. Functional
        i. Cabinets
        ii. Drawers
    c. Display – countertops
2. Professional – work
    a. Essential – desk
    b. Interactive – credenza and office file cabinets
    c. Destination – storage file cabinets and shelves

RETENTION PLAN - SPACE

1. Design it
2. Use appropriate containers
3. Make it easily accessible

RELOCATION PLAN - STUFF

1. Discard it
2. Donate it
   a. Salvation Army
   b. Goodwill
   c. Local shelter
3. Pass it on
   a. Family
   b. Friends
4. Sell it
5. Cancel it
   a. Unnecessary subscriptions
   b. Memberships
6. File it

THE KEYS

1. Inventory from the outside in
2. Implement a replacement strategy
3. File all paper

Follow the talent you have been given.

MANAGING YOUR FILES

ACTION FILES

1. To Tickler
2. To Route
3. To Read
4. To File

TICKLER FILES

1. Daily – 1 to 31
2. Miscellaneous – January to December

To manage priorities, you must
first know what they are.

INTERACTIVE FILING SYSTEMS

1. Alphabetic
2. Numeric
3. Subject
   a. Dictionary
   b. Encyclopedic
      i. Primary – file guides
      ii. Secondary – hanging file folders
      iii. Tertiary – file folders

FINDING THE LOST FILE

1. Look in files immediately in front or behind of the original correct location
2. Look between files
3. Look in the bottom of the file drawer
4. Check in, on, or around the copying and fax machines
5. Check in the break room or coffee area
6. Email coworkers
7. Check the "office pack rats" work area

Give some people an inch and
they think they're a ruler

MANAGING YOUR PAPER

LEAVE NOTHING "HOMELESS"

1. Trash it
2. File it
3. Purge it

HANDLING INCOMING MAIL

1. If possible, assign a person to sort through your mail, weeding out any junk mail that you still are receiving
2. Process your mail at the same time each day – standing
3. Get your name off of mailing lists
   a. Direct Mail Association
   b. Credit Bureau Association
   c. Bureaus "opt out"
4. Don't open it if your name is misspelled or your title is wrong
5. File it or trash it

Give without remembering;
receive without forgetting.

HANDLING INCOMING CORRESPONDENCE

1. Move your incoming tray off of your desk – get it out of your line of sight

2. Process your incoming tray twice daily – standing

3. File it or trash it

4. Have the necessary support pieces in close proximity to your incoming tray

   a. Waste basket

   b. Action files

   c. Miscellaneous tickler files

PAPERS ITEMS THAT BURY YOUR DESK

1. Items you need to act on

2. Items someone else needs to act on

3. Items of interest

4. Items that need filed

5. Items you don't know what to do with

6. Items that are useless

I would rather see a sermon than hear one.

MANAGING YOUR TECHNOLOGY

FAX MACHINE

1. Your fax machine should be programmable and provide you with clear copies

2. Position it in close proximity to your incoming correspondence tray

3. Educate personnel on usage regarding incoming and outgoing faxes

4. Check your fax machine only during scheduled intervals and, if possible, have someone place your faxes in your incoming tray – don't stand by it

VOICE MAIL

1. When you leave or respond to a message, you should outline your main points prior to leaving the message

2. Introduce yourself and state your objective

3. Educate your colleagues that you check your voice mail daily at regular designated times (maximum of three)

4. Be clear, concise, state all numbers slowly, and repeat numbers

5. If a response is required, let them know when you're available

6. You should have specific instructions on your voice mail outlining how a person can transfer to someone else for immediate action

7. Your voice mail system should have a capacity to hold only ten 90-second messages

EMAIL

1. Create an email policy and enforce it

    a. Hardware/software databases are proprietary, which reinforces why there should be no personal usage

    b. Audit the database every six months

    c. Include the policy in the handbook and explain the penalty for violations

2. Determine how you want them to respond

3. Don't let email linger in your mailbox – read it, act on anything that you can handle immediately in two minutes or less, file it, or delete it as soon as possible

4. Set up two action folders for items requiring more than two minutes of focused attention: "Read" folder and "Reply" folder

5. Don't cc everyone in the company – the more you send, the more you receive

6. When replying, omit the original text – if the sender can't remember the original message, how important was it?

7. Avoid the routine email – thank-you notes and FYI

8. Be responsible – never send a message you wouldn't want to receive yourself or one that you wouldn't want your supervisor to see

9. Turn off the indicator – only check your email at designated times (maximum of three)

10. Keep the messages short – use the subject line and attach documents

INTERNET

1. Monitor – communicate and specify scope and frequency

2. Limit personal use to before, after work, or during lunch

3. Outline disciplinary action in detail

4. Block inappropriate site access

MANAGING YOUR MEETINGS

REASON

1. Exchange information
2. Solve problems
3. Brainstorm new ideas
4. Educate
5. Develop plans and programs

PEOPLE

1. Leader
2. Facilitator
3. Recorder
4. Time Keeper
5. Participants

AGENDA

1. Objective – clearly defined
2. Discussion items – provided by participants
3. Time limits – discussion items
4. Breaks – preassigned

If you fail to plan, you're planning to fail.

CHECKLIST

1. Pre-meeting
   a. Distribute agenda a few days prior to the meeting
   b. Attach a memo to the agenda that includes the meeting objective, date, time, location, and attendees
   c. Encourage agenda sponsors to plan their parts
   d. Determine the cost
2. Meeting
   a. Begin on time
   b. Keep focused on objective and discussion items
   c. Maintain a parking lot
   d. Develop action plan
      i. Action
      ii. Person responsible
      iii. Deadline
   e. Summarize action plan and pass out meeting evaluation form
   f. Finish on time
3. Post-meeting
   a. Evaluations – returned within 24 hours
   b. Action plan – distribute to attendees within three days

MANAGING YOUR PLAN

COMMIT TO MAKING NECESSARY CHANGES

1. Purpose_____

2. Attitude_____

3. Stress_____

4. Relationships_____

5. Responsibilities_____

6. Activities_____

7. Space_____

8. Files_____

9. Paper_____

10. Technology_____

11. Meetings_____

Plan filling in the above eleven and making the commitment

KEYS TO MAKING CHANGES

1. Write them down – give them to a friend in an envelope

2. Establish deadlines

3. Monitor your progress – know your parameters

4. Make yourself accountable – have a friend mail them the changes to you in six months

5. Write down the potential obstacles – what might get worse

6. Make a list of the resources necessary to make the changes – utilize the resources you have

LIFE-BALANCING QUESTIONS

1. What part of your internal balance needs improvement?
2. What part of your external balance needs improvement?
3. Do your actions match your answers?

LIFE-BALANCING BENEFITS

1. Richer relationships
2. Longer life
3. Happiness
4. Enjoyment
5. Inner peace

If you want to be respected, you have
to like what you see in the mirror.

PERSONAL ACTION PLAN

1. What impacted you the most in this chapter on Organization and how will it change the way you manage multiple priorites?

    _____

    _____

    _____

    _____

    _____

    _____

2. Specifically, how & what are you going to do, based on #1 above?

    _____

    _____

    _____

    _____

    _____

    _____

3. Who are you going to be accountable to?

    _____

    _____

    _____

    _____

    _____

    _____

*The purpose of this action plan is to help make certain
that by reading this chapter it produces a positive change
in the way you manage multiple priorities.*

CUSTOMER SERVICE

Serving 2 Succeed

A true customer focus, a true service focus, requires a fairly fundamental re-learning process that goes to the deepest levels of the organizational culture. It requires an open and honest effort to discern the truth of customer value and an aggressive determination to implement it in a very thorough way.

All of us still have much to learn if we are to move our organizations beyond the level of slogans and platitudes about customer service. Nearly two decades after the publication of Service America!, which launched a so-called service revolution in the USA and eventually abroad, can we really say most of our businesses, hospitals, and schools are truly customer focused? Just consult your own recent experience and you'll see that most of the real opportunities still lie before us.

No matter what you sell – products or services or a combination of both – the problems you face are still the same. How do I create, market, and sell our products or services to the best of my ability? How do I hire, train, and keep the best employees to help us reach this goal? What is the best way to organize my company so it runs smoothly? How do I manage the money, the costs, the inventory, and the physical and psychological assets that make up our organization?

Amidst all of these questions comes several important ones: How do I attract, serve, and keep customers? And if it's true that in business nothing happens until somebody sells something to somebody, it's even more true that no business can survive unless it directs all its efforts towards serving the people who ultimately do the buying – the customers. Unless the strategies, systems, and the service employees are centered on the needs and expectations of the customer, the organization will not thrive. It is time to turn your organization into a customer-focused entity and *start serving to succeed.*

> Sometimes you have to stumble
> to prevent falling.

SERVICE BARRIERS

NOT UNDERSTANDING THE IMPORTANCE OF EXCEPTIONAL CUSTOMER SERVICE

1. Sixty-eight percent of those customers who switch products and/or services do so because of the manner in which they were treated

2. Only 10% switch because of the dissatisfaction of the product and/or service

3. Taking care of the customer means taking care of business

4. The strength of the organization is dependent on customer service

5. The strength of customer service is dependent on continuous learning by the people who deliver it

NOT UNDERSTANDING THE CUSTOMER SERVICE CHAIN

1. In your position you are either dealing directly with the customer or someone who does—chain reaction

2. Everyone in the organization impacts the customer service chain

3. Certain jobs or positions have the greatest opportunity to influence or retain customers

4. Everyone from the President and CEO to the Customer Service Representative has customers—if you're not serving the customer directly, serve someone who is

NOT UNDERSTANDING THE VALUE OF A CUSTOMER

1. A customer is the most important person in any business

2. A customer is not dependent on us

3. A customer is the purpose of our work

4. A customer does us a favor when they do business with us

5. A customer is a person who brings us their needs

6. A customer makes it possible to pay our salaries

7. A customer is the life blood of any business

NOT UNDERSTANDING WHY CUSTOMERS FIRE YOU

1. Showing no genuine or personal interest – impersonal service and insincere people

2. Poor response – some people will sacrifice quality for speed

3. Unavailability of people or product – when they can't get the stuff they need or reach the person they want, they'll go someplace else

4. Hard to conduct business or order – computer voice attendant rather than a real human being answers the phone

5. Unfriendly person on the front line – smile

6. Overpromising – when you overpromise and under-deliver, you lose

7. Poor professional package or image – customers want to feel that the quality of their business will be reflected by the quality of those they deal with

8. Nickel-and-diming – charging for incidentals such as copies, phone calls, and interest on late payments

9. Poor product quality – no matter how much people pay, they expect a quality product

10. Poor or rude collection practices – keeping the customer is as important as collecting the money

---

Enthusiasm makes everything different.

SERVICE CULTURE

MISSION

1. Who we are as an organization
2. What we are as an organization
3. Why we exist as an organization
4. Where we are headed as an organization
5. How we are going to get there as an organization

VALUES

1. Respect – treat everyone with dignity, and value different backgrounds, cultures, and viewpoints
2. Integrity – honesty, consistency, and professionalism in every facet of your behavior
3. Teamwork – work and communicate across functions, levels, geographies, and business units to build the organization; hold each other accountable for behavior and performance
4. Innovation – challenge yourselves by embracing innovation and creativity, not only in your products and services but also in all aspects of your work; learn from both your successes and failures
5. Quality – deliver the quality and craftsmanship that consumers demand

What you permit, you promote.

OBJECTIVES

1. Exceptional service – provide world-class service with personal concern for our customers and our team

2. Financial strength – to maintain a superior financial position and inspire the complete trust and confidence of our customers

3. Operational excellence – to deliver exceptional value to our customers through operational excellence

4. Unified team – to cultivate a highly motivated and committed team that embodies the organization's values

5. Innovative products and services – to meet our customers' needs

6. Market development – to develop and enhance the real and intrinsic long-term value of our customers

CUSTOMER-FOCUSED

1. Leadership spend at least 20% of their time meeting with customers

2. Formal customer research is conducted at least once a year

3. Meetings with customers regularly involve people from several departments

4. Customers regularly rate you on service

5. Customer satisfaction is a key role in evaluating leadership performance

6. Management meetings devote as much time to customers needs as they do to internal issues

7. Routinely partner with customers to solve problems

8. Staying in constant touch with customers rather than waiting until they have a problem

DEFINING YOUR CUSTOMER

WHO ARE YOUR CUSTOMERS?

1. Existing customers – those who are doing business with you now

2. New customers – coming into contact with your organization for the first or second time

3. Potential customers – everyone who isn't your customer

   a. Advertising – direct mail

   b. Referrals – service excellence

   c. Location

   d. Price

   e. Accidentally or by chance

4. Internal customers – people who work in your organization and do business with each other

THE CUSTOMER'S MOMENTS OF TRUTH

1. Moment of truth – first contact and first impression

2. Interim moments of truth – the service experience continues

3. Final moment of truth – the customer has completed business with you and is ready to grade the experience

---

Nothing happens without
well-timed reminders.

THE CUSTOMER'S OUTLOOK

1. Betrayed – once loyal but now committed to damaging your reputation

2. Angry – had a bad experience and now actively rejects you because they feel you owe them more than compensation

3. Disappointed – has no intention of working with you again and does not trust you

4. Stranger – has heard of you but has no opinion about you and what makes you different from the rest

5. Acquaintance – doing business with you but has no strong opinion and may only do business when the offer is good enough

6. Loyal – returns to you again and again, buys your latest products and/or services, and is willing to pay even more because of the service

7. Advocate – mentions you positively to friends and colleagues and will write a testimonial letter if you ask

8. Ambassador – actively promotes you by making introductions and enthusiastic recommendations

HOW CUSTOMERS IMPACT YOUR BUSINESS

1. More transactions

2. More dollars per transaction

SERVICE GUIDELINES

KEEP THE CUSTOMER'S BEST INTEREST IN MIND

1. Focus on your customer's needs and ask "How can I help?" instead of "What can I sell?"

2. Ask questions to find out exactly what they need
   a. What types of issues are we facing?
   b. Can you describe what happened?
   c. What do you need in order to do this?
   d. If the customer knows what he or she needs, get it

3. Give them what they want (need), not what you think they ought to have – no assuming and no forced agenda

4. Be honest with them about "wait times" such as appointments, shipments, and anything that requires them to wait for service

5. Don't be afraid to send them to the competition if the assessment warrants it

6. Watch out for them with regard to quantity, cost, and even the best way to ship your product

SERVE THEM BY USING YOUR ACE

1. Attentive to their requests

2. Caring about their needs

3. Excited about your services and products

> Problems provide the paycheck
> that customers sign.

EARN THE RIGHT TO ASK FOR MORE

1. Always confirm appointments – they appreciate the reminder

2. Develop a relationship before you address the customer's request or attempt to ask him or her for anything

3. Use the customer's name and encourage him or her to use yours – people always prefer to do business with someone they know

4. Replicate the very best experience you have ever had as a customer

5. See each customer as unique as you try to understand his or her needs, issues, and concerns

6. Look for opportunities to compliment the customer

7. Look for things you have in common with the customer

8. Be time sensitive – follow up when a deadline is involved

9. Throw in an extra – everyone likes to get more than expected

WORKING HARD TO KEEP THEM

1. Contact each customer after the sale to ensure satisfaction with the product or service and verify that it was correct, on time, and in excellent condition

2. After you resolve a customer's problem, follow up to ensure everything is okay

3. Ask customers how they would like to be served and contacted and give them a choice between phone, fax, or email

4. Send email and/or faxes each day notifying customers of their shipment and how it was shipped – tracking number if possible

5. Send a personalized thank-you note for their business with no agenda or purpose

6. Send handwritten notes to all key customers notifying them of special events or promotions

SERVICE STRATEGIES

BUILD SOLID RELATIONSHIPS

1. Give value: give value to customers, not facts about you
2. Tell truths: tell the truth even if it hurts or embarrasses you
3. Beat goals: customers are attracted to achievers
4. Gain knowledge: collect as much knowledge about customers as you do about your company and your product or service
5. Have answers: build your credibility as an information resource rather than as a salesperson
6. Tell stories: stories are personal, revealing, and help people relate
7. Tell how: what to do isn't as important as how to do it
8. Build value: gets customers leads or put them in front of contacts that might lead them to business
9. Find links: find something in common that ties you together

---

> Perspective is the way you see it, the way
> you want it, and the way it really is.

FOCUS ON "WHAT'S RIGHT"

1. View complaints as a second chance to impress customers
2. Never tell a customer what you can't do; their only interest is what you can do
3. The customer isn't always right, but it's never our job to prove the customer wrong

BE UNIQUE IN YOUR APPROACH

1. Dare to be different – risk success
2. Dare to try something new – risk failure

PRACTICE THE FIVE P'S

1. Passion – love what you do, why you do it, and who you do it with
2. Prepared – you can claim to be surprised once; after that, you're unprepared
3. Polite – friendly and considerate no matter what kind of day you're having
4. Prompt – never keep a member waiting without acknowledging them
5. Present – your members want to be treated as individuals, not the next task

---

Become an expert in the impossible.

VALUE-ADDED SERVICE

VALUES THAT HAVE NOTHING TO DO WITH PRICE

1. Quality service to all customers
2. Product quality
3. Warranties or money-back guarantees
4. Service or installation after the sale
5. Industry leadership
6. Reputation for quality from satisfied customers
7. Reliability that extends through the company to products and services
8. Unique desire to do what is right for the customer every time

FOLLOW UP

1. Current events – customer's locale
2. Industry information pertinent to their organization
3. Encouragement notes and cards
4. Logo items
5. Membership and rewards program
6. Private numbers
7. Celebrate service accomplishments – literature

Success is measured by your
reaction to adversity.

BE EASY TO DO BUSINESS WITH

1. Convenient business hours – survey your customers
2. Provide a service guarantee – if not met, give them something
3. Provide options – payment preference, shipping, ordering
4. Network luncheon for local customers
5. Frequent buyers club – discounts, gifts, free products
6. Customer directory – circulate and encourage customers to use
7. Take advantage of technology
    a. Phone system that has a provision to talk with someone
    b. Toll-free number
    c. After-hours answering system – return call the next day
    d. 24-hour emergency number
    e. Lose the music – benefit messages
    f. Utilize contact management software
    g. Utilize electronic greeting cards and newsletters
    h. Cyber network – bulletin board on your web site

Adversity is inevitable... misery is optional.

FEAST ON CUSTOMER FEEDBACK

1. Email direct to owner/president
2. Customer advisory board – key clients that meet quarterly
3. Customer service survey – continue/stop/start

If you are not serving the customer,
serve someone who is.

MASTERING YOUR MESSAGE

WHAT INFLUENCES YOUR MESSAGE

1. Face-to-face communication
    a. Body language – 55%
    b. Tone of voice – 38%
    c. Words – 7%
2. Telephone communication
    a. Tone of voice – 82%
    b. Words – 18%

VOCAL QUALITIES

1. Tone – expresses feeling or emotion
2. Inflection – emphasizing words and syllables to enhance your message
3. Pitch – how high or deep your voice sounds
4. Rate – how many words spoken per minute
5. Volume – how loud or soft your voice sounds
6. Articulation – quality and clarity of words spoken

Life is tough... compared to what?

PHONE ETIQUETTE

1. Putting a caller on hold
   a. Explain why
   b. Ask permission
   c. Put the caller on hold
   d. Thank the caller for holding
2. Transferring a call
   a. Tell the caller to whom he or she will be transferred
   b. Explain why
   c. Ask permission
   d. Give the phone number and extension in case of disconnection
   e. Transfer the call

TEN MOST IMPORTANT WORDS TO A CUSTOMER

1. Their own name
2. Yes
3. Thank you
4. Glad you're here
5. How may I serve you
6. What is most convenient for you
7. What else can I do for you
8. I'm not sure but I will find out
9. Thank you for your business – please come back again
10. I apologize for our mistake – let me make it right

HANDLING TOUGH CUSTOMERS

PREPARE YOURSELF

1. View problems as opportunities
2. Be prepared to listen
3. See the customer's perspective first
4. Own the problem
5. Put the problem in context
6. Breathe

LEAP INTO RESOLUTION

1. Listen and let them vent
2. Endure and stay calm
3. Acknowledge and mirror the customer's feelings
4. Pamper their emotions and remain focused

A star shines the most when it is the darkest.

DON'T ESCALATE THE SITUATION

1. Never interrupt – listen first before you try to reason

2. Never argue – remember, your job is not to prove them wrong

3. Never assume – respect the customer's perceptions as real to him or her

4. Never quote your policies – some policies look better on paper than in practice

ACTION STEPS

1. Accept responsibility – you are "they"

2. Takes notes – focus on key points

3. Use "I" instead of "you" – "what can I do?" instead of "what do you need?"

4. Be agreeable – acknowledge their problem

5. Stay focused – your job is to meet the customer's needs

You must turn your back to the crowd
in order for people to follow.

ONLINE SERVICE

GAINING THE CUSTOMER'S TRUST

1. Total security
2. Don't offer goods and services that are not available elsewhere
3. Over-communicate information to avoid unanswered questions
4. Be available 24/7
5. Build a system with seamless integration and user-friendly access

MEETING CUSTOMER NEEDS

1. Organize content to ease decision-making
2. Provide simple product and service descriptions
3. Facilitate various forms of contact
4. Support the product and services with inventory levels that guarantee fulfillment
5. Use an automated workflow tracking and strive for the lowest possible error rate
6. Make everything quick, pleasant, and effortless

Desire more than you can accomplish.

EMAIL PROCEDURES

1. Use software that prioritizes messages by date and lets the sender know the message has reached the proper department

2. Track the email questions you get and gear your answers to meet the specific needs of your customers

3. Provide links to let people pursue more detailed information

4. Offer recipients an easy way to unsubscribe with every electronic message you send

5. Make sure all outgoing email is useful, timely, and personalized

6. Never forget that email is a legal document

7. Train employees to convey an email message that keeps the human touch

UNFRIENDLY PRACTICES

1. Making it difficult for customers to navigate and find what they want

2. Treating customers anonymously

3. Teasing them with information that requires more detail

4. Designing a system without regard for customer needs

5. Making promises you can't deliver and being the answer to everything

6. Disregarding the coordination and sharing of information among various departments in the organization

PERFORMANCE MEASURES

VIDEO REPORT CARD

1. First impression – be smiling
2. Acknowledge customers immediately – 100% attention
3. Customers awaiting a response – may I help the next person?
4. Tell them your name and use their name often
5. Sixty-second hold limit – give a status report
6. Don't transfer a call without an introduction of the caller
7. Body language – install mirrors for reflective behavior
8. Restate important information
9. Always thank a customer
10. Always invite them back

SERVICE HABITS

1. Greet the customer
2. Value the customer
3. Find out what the customer wants
4. Help the customer
5. Invite the customer back

Men are from earth, women are
from earth... deal with it.

PERFORMANCE INDICATORS

1. Teamwork
2. Attitude
3. Customer service (internal and external)
4. Promoting company success

CRITICAL SUCCESS FACTORS

1. Did I think of myself as a customer service professional today?
2. Did I maintain a positive attitude about my customers?
3. Did I provide excellent service to my internal customers and my company?
4. Did I work to build rapport and relationships with all my customers?
5. Was I able to ask good questions to better understand what my customers wanted?
6. Did I listen carefully to everything my customers said?
7. Was I able to offer more products, services, or options to my customers?
8. Did I handle complaints and difficult customers calmly and professionally?
9. Was I able to exceed my customers' expectations most of the time?

Clarity is the perspective you can't see.

RECRUITING THE BEST

TOP TEN TRAITS OF CUSTOMER SERVICE PROFESSIONALS

1. Optimism and enthusiasm
2. A positive mental image
3. A competitive spirit
4. A social disposition
5. An inquisitive mind
6. Organization
7. Respect
8. Accurate decision making
9. Communication
10. Knowledge

CHARACTERISTICS OF AN EFFECTIVE INTERVIEW

1. Interviewee does 85% of the talking
2. Interviewer is assertive and engaging
3. Interviewer takes notes
4. Interviewer does not sell the position
5. Interviewer does not use the applicant's resume or job application to interview from
6. Interviewer probes desired qualities and behavior from a list of prepared questions

---

Self-improvement focus leaves
no time for criticism.

PROBING PRINCIPLES

1. Ask general and ambiguous questions
2. Ask value judgment questions, not factual – what did you like least...?
3. Probe choice points and unusual situations – if you could have either...?
4. Ask questions unrelated to interviewee's experience or jobs

"GETTING TO KNOW YOU" PROBES

1. If you could invite a well-known person to lunch, who would that be?
2. State an embarrassing moment in your life
3. What is your favorite book or Broadway play?
4. If you worked for you, what would be your number one constructive criticism?
5. Would winning one million dollars change your daily routine?
6. What would you like to be your legacy?

Always be learning.

RETAINING THE BEST

MAKE THE RIGHT IMPRESSION FIRST

1. What would impress you if you were a new employee?
2. What information would you want to have?
3. What information would you absolutely need?
4. Who would you like to meet?
5. What would make you feel like an accepted member of the team?

CREATING A BETTER WORKPLACE

1. Hire happy people – you don't have enough time to teach happy
2. Provide a supportive work atmosphere – remove all threatening signs and turn "no" into a more gentle reminder
3. Ask them what they think – solicit regular feedback and reward the best idea of the month
4. Provide "I care" benefits – event tickets, AAA memberships, resources
5. Make people feel valuable – honor a different employee every week
6. Party – celebrate everything you can

> I would rather be questioned for what I am, than believed for what I am not.

ELEMENTS TO ENSURE EMPLOYEE COMMITMENT

1. Balance between work and family life
2. Organizational direction
3. Growth opportunities
4. Recognition and rewards
5. Job satisfaction
6. Work environment

GROWING YOUR SERVICE CULTURE

1. Develop leadership – gain buy-in
2. Recruit the right people
3. Communicate the service vision
4. Provide continuous training
5. Establish sales and service goals
6. Monitor performance – what gets measured gets done
7. Reward performance – create incentive programs

Attitude doesn't solve problems, it
only determines the outcome.

PERSONAL ACTION PLAN

1. What impacted you the most in this chapter on Customer Service and how will it change the way you serve your customers?

_____

_____

_____

_____

_____

_____

2. Specifically, how & what are you going to do, based on #1 above?

_____

_____

_____

_____

_____

_____

3. Who are you going to be accountable to?

_____

_____

_____

_____

_____

_____

_____

The purpose of this action plan is to help make certain that by reading this chapter it produces a positive change in the way you serve your customers.

Assessments & Resources

SELF-ASSESSMENT

Please answer the following statements either "yes" or "no."

1. I have a valid opinion of myself and am aware of my positive qualities without arrogance or conceit. Yes ☐ No ☐

2. I possess the attributes of enthusiasm, patience, perseverance and adaptability. Yes ☐ No ☐

3. As a part of my daily routine, I know and practice the importance of caring for and preserving my health. Yes ☐ No ☐

4. I plan ahead and take one step at a time to achieve my goals through a series of small steady actions. Yes ☐ No ☐

5. I am careful to store up useful knowledge in my subconscious by monitoring what I see, hear, read and experience. Yes ☐ No ☐

6. Fear or ridicule create a barrier to my creative potential and ingenuity. Yes ☐ No ☐

7. My associates are goal-oriented individuals who are willing to take risks to succeed and are very positive people. Yes ☐ No ☐

8. I am willing to try different approaches to solving a problem and take advantage of an opportunity. Yes ☐ No ☐

9. I have strength and determination when developing habits and would consider my habits to be good. Yes ☐ No ☐

10. I expect to succeed and remain optimistic about the outcome of my goals despite temporary disappointments. Yes ☐ No ☐

CULTURE ASSESSMENT

Complete this assessment to identify the components necessary to energize people and create a culture conducive to growth. Circle only one answer for each question.

1. To recognize the value of employees, the company's leadership must:
   a. Assess their skills.
   b. Look at their contributions.
   c. Measure what their work contributes to the bottom line.

2. If people feel valued as contributors to a company, it usually leads to:
   a. Financial results.
   b. A fun work environment.
   c. Less rumor mill.

3. Embodied within a mission statement should be:
   a. A statement of objectives with a cause.
   b. A statement of objectives that include customer awareness.
   c. A statement of objectives that are simple to understand.

4. Creating a culture that promotes personal growth is important because:
   a. People will be content.
   b. Employees will be loyal.
   c. You can no longer promise job security.

5. Key to a motivating work environment is to:
   a. Have regular training sessions.
   b. Give employees recognition.
   c. Allow flex time.

6. All successful companies work toward:
   a. Creating and keeping customers.
   b. Quarterly profit.
   c. Growth.

7. An effective way to strengthen workers' productivity is to:
   a. Keep track of measured results.
   b. Establish a manager-worker partnership.
   c. Set specific goals.

8. Even the most ambitious and hard-working employees can become demotivated by:
   a. Bureaucracy of a company.
   b. Too much focus on the bottom line.
   c. Management style different than theirs.

9. Innovation as a company value should be demonstrated by:
   a. People who act on their ideas while taking ownership of results.
   b. People who take risks on a regular basis.
   c. People who try new ways even if they do not have the expertise in the subject.

10. A learning organization should lead to:
   a. More training dollars spent on skills and competencies.
   b. A more intelligent work force.
   c. A teaching organization.

COMMUNICATION ASSESSMENT

Rate yourself on a scale of 1 to 5 in regard to each of the following statements, with 1 being "strongly disagree" and 5 being "strongly agree."

_____ 1. As a matter of personal pride, I take special care of my clothing and grooming.

_____ 2. My posture and carriage are erect and forceful.

_____ 3. I make good eye contact with people I talk to.

_____ 4. I enjoy public speaking, and my friends think I'm a good storyteller.

_____ 5. When I have an important statement to make, I write it out first.

_____ 6. When I write out my speech or statement, I try to anticipate questions or answers from my audience.

_____ 7. I keep my work area neat and clean as an example to my coworkers.

_____ 8. When I schedule a meeting, I'm the first one to arrive at the meeting area so I can take advantage of last minute details.

_____ 9. I constantly look for different ways to get my message across to my constituents in a positive fashion.

_____ 10. I always make certain that those I communicate with understand exactly what I want to get across.

Add up all the numbers in each box.   Score: _____

PROFICIENCY PROFILE ASSESSMENT

Rate yourself on some of the key characteristics of leaders. Using a scale of 1 to 5 (1 being the lowest and 5 the highest), write the number you feel best describes your ability as it relates to each of the characteristics.

_____ 1. Honest

_____ 2. Vision-oriented

_____ 3. Inspirational

_____ 4. Competent

_____ 5. Communicate and listen well

_____ 6. Dependable

_____ 7. Consistent

_____ 8. Self-confident

_____ 9. Fair-minded

_____ 10. Open to ideas of others

_____ 11. Motivating

_____ 12. Assertive

_____ 13. Recognize the positive behaviors and accomplishments of others

_____ 14. Problem solver/decision maker

_____ 15. Goal-oriented

_____ 16. Change-oriented

_____ 17. Effectively manage time

_____ 18. People-oriented

_____ 19. Able to deal with many issues

_____ 20. Seek knowledge

PATHWAYS TO LEADERSHIP

Leadership isn't about titles, positions, or flowcharts. Leadership is influence. Your influence potential will determine your leadership potential. It is critical to have people following you because they want to, not because they feel they have to. To accomplish that, begin by doing the following.

Lead – by focusing on your people, not your bottom line. Managers manage things and leaders lead people. Your goal shouldn't be to build a big bottom line, but to develop good people. People quickly figure out whether you are leading them or using them.

Enlarge – by adding value to a person. People will always move toward anyone who enlarges them. People are dynamic and must be led through love and relationship. A good leader is a person who can step on your toes without messing up your shine.

Appreciate – by never taking anyone or anything for granted. You cannot maintain high quality people and products unless they are managed with compassion and care. Leadership is caring about people and appreciating their efforts.

Model – by always doing whatever it takes. People will listen to what you say but will be influenced by what you do. Your actions must match your beliefs, or as someone once said, "I'd rather see a sermon than hear one."

Enthusiastic – by making sure your attitude outdistances your abilities. When you learn from others, assist others and have fun doing it, you will have more enthusiasm for what you do. People are mesmerized by power, but moved by enthusiasm.

Grow – by focusing on improvement, not just achievement. As a leader you tend to set "the" bar and only recognize those people who go above it. You tend to recognize and confront negative behavior more often and in a bigger way than you do any type of positive behavior. Begin to recognize and reward improvement and watch them grow.

Solve – by allowing your mistakes to stretch you, not stop you. A leader must be big enough to admit their mistakes, smart enough to profit from them, and strong enough to correct them. Teach people to resolve problems, not to endure them.

Credible – by doing the right thing, at the right time, for the right reason. An infrastructure of great character is built from the top down. The trust of your followers is directly proportionate and parallel to the level of your own character.

Involvement – by caring enough to know and knowing enough to care. It is good when people believe in their leader, but it is better when the leader believes in the people. To know them is to trust them. Make sure you know who you're leading.

Mentor – by making everything a process and not an event. Failing allows you to mentor and begin again more intelligently. If a mistake is not immoral or fundamentally undermining to the direction of the organization, view it as a learning experience and an investment for your future.

Steve Gilliland has the tools to equip you on your journey to acquiring the essentials necessary for improving performance:

DVDS

Enjoy The Ride
Making a Difference

CD SETS

A Treasury of Motivation (6 CDs)
Steve Gilliland Collection (6 CDs)

CDS

Dealing with Negative Attitudes in the Workplace
Enjoy The Ride
Hits of Humor
Leading with Heart
Making a Difference
On The Air

BOOKS

The Five Principles of Leadership
A License to Chill
Enjoy The Ride
Mum's The Word
Performance Essentials in the Workplace

AUDIO BOOKS

Enjoy The Ride (Unabridged, 2 CDs)
Mum's The Word (Unabridged, 3 CDs)

For more information or to order, visit
www.impactstore.com

TreeNeutral™

Advantage Media Group is proud to be a part of the Tree Neutral™ program. Tree Neutral offsets the number of trees consumed in the production and printing of this book by taking proactive steps such as planting trees in direct proportion to the number of trees used to print books. To learn more about Tree Neutral, please visit **www.treeneutral. com.** To learn more about Advantage Media Group's commitment to being a responsible steward of the environment, please visit **www. advantagefamily.com/green**

Performance Essentials in the Workplace is available in bulk quantities at special discounts for corporate, institutional, and educational purposes. To learn more about the special programs Advantage Media Group offers, please visit **www. KaizenUniversity.com** or call 1.866.775.1696.

Advantage Media Group is a leading publisher of business, motivation, and self-help authors. Do you have a manuscript or book idea that you would like to have considered for publication? Please visit **www.amgbook.com**

CPSIA information can be obtained at www.ICGtesting.com
Printed in the USA
BVOW050634111111

275875BV00007B/2/P